A Disney PRINCESS Journey Through History

By Courtney B. Carbone

Illustrated by the Disney Storybook Art Team

Random House New York

Contents

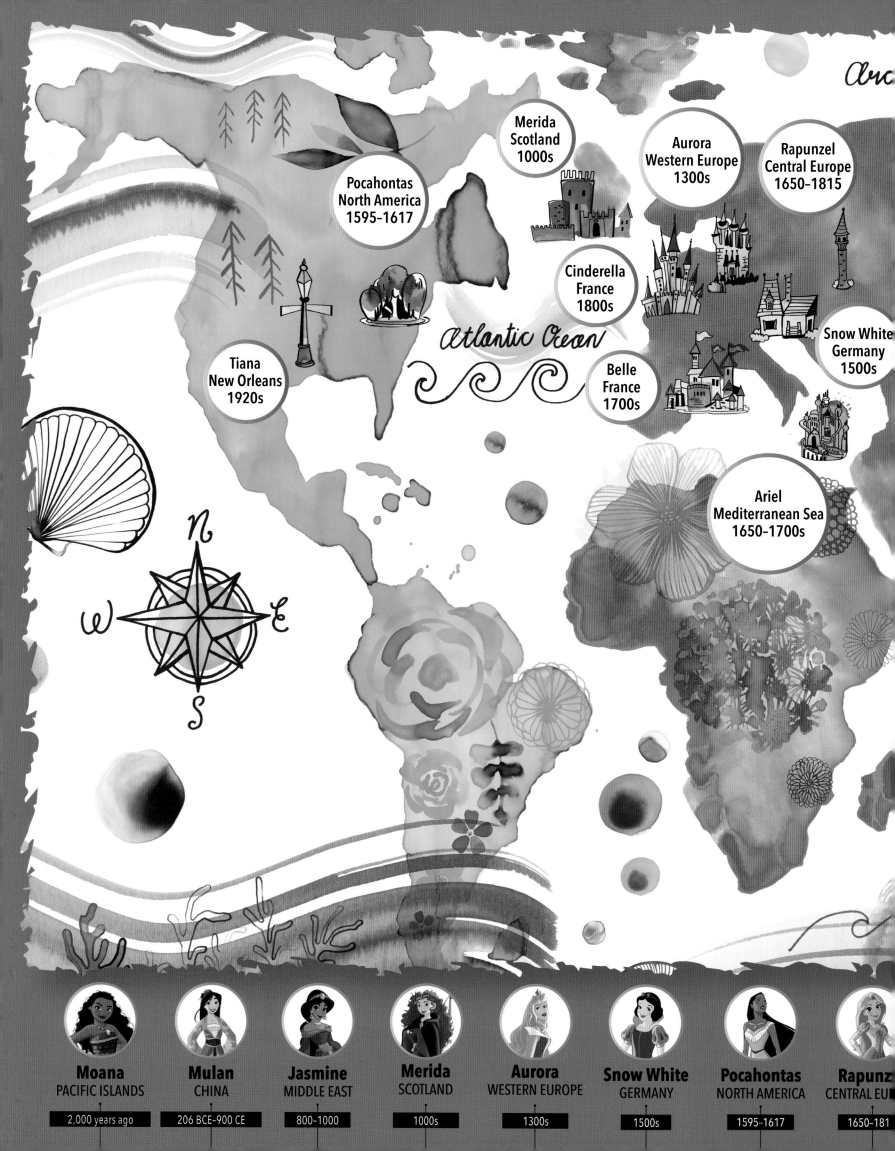

Merida
Scotland
1000s

Aurora
Western Europe
1300s

Rapunzel
Central Europe
1650–1815

Pocahontas
North America
1595–1617

Cinderella
France
1800s

Snow White
Germany
1500s

Atlantic Ocean

Belle
France
1700s

Tiana
New Orleans
1920s

Ariel
Mediterranean Sea
1650–1700s

Moana
PACIFIC ISLANDS
2,000 years ago

Mulan
CHINA
206 BCE–900 CE

Jasmine
MIDDLE EAST
800–1000

Merida
SCOTLAND
1000s

Aurora
WESTERN EUROPE
1300s

Snow White
GERMANY
1500s

Pocahontas
NORTH AMERICA
1595–1617

Rapunzel
CENTRAL EUROPE
1650–181

Disney Princess Overview

Jasmine
Middle East
800-1000

Pacific Ocean

Mulan
China
206 BCE-900 CE

Moana
Pacific Islands
2,000 years ago

Indian Ocean

A NOTE TO THE READER

As you may already know, many of the Disney Princess characters are based on old stories and legends. While the Disney Princesses and their stories may have drawn inspiration from different historical events and locations, none of them, with the exception of Pocahontas, actually lived in any of these places or time periods.

Ariel
ERRANEAN SEA

Belle
FRANCE

Cinderella
FRANCE

Tiana
NEW ORLEANS

650-1700s

1700s

1800s

1920s

What Is a Princess?

While the Disney Princesses live in areas inspired by a variety of places, cultures, and time periods, they have many similar qualities and characteristics. For example, Moana and Tiana worked hard to find their place in the world and achieve their dreams—even though they were born thousands of years apart. And although Mulan and Merida have very different personalities, neither allowed society's expectations to define them.

Here are some other qualities and values that the princesses have in common:

Bravery

Strength of self

Being true to their heart

Love of animals

Doing the right thing

Sense of adventure

Challenging expectations

Loyalty to family

Treasuring friendship

Society doesn't define them

Working hard

Caring for others

Dreaming big

But you don't need to be a princess to have these qualities!
Anyone can be bold, dream big, and find adventure.

Read on to find out more about the Disney Princesses!

Did You Know?

Throughout the book, be on the lookout for Did You Know? boxes to learn even more history. And if you don't know the meaning of a word or a term, check out the glossary on the next pages for some helpful explanations!

Words to Know: A Glossary Before the Journey

Age of Enlightenment: a period in the seventeenth and eighteenth centuries during which culture, philosophy, and education flourished throughout Europe, resulting in great advancements in the arts and in civilization as a whole

BCE: stands for Before Common Era; the period of time before year 0 CE (Common Era)

Brothers Grimm, The: German brothers Jacob and Wilhelm Grimm, who lived during the eighteenth and nineteenth centuries, and are known for their collection of folktales, which includes the stories of Snow White, Rapunzel, Cinderella, and many more

chain mail: protective armor made from small metal rings that are interconnected

chemise: a smocklike undergarment worn under a dress

court: the royal family or household

damask: richly patterned fabric

dynasty: a family that rules over a region for a long period of time

flying buttresses: individual structure underpinnings that provide support to tall, thin stone walls

genealogy: the history of a family and their ancestors, or the study of family history

humanism: the focus on the everyday lives of human beings instead of a divine or supernatural power

indigenous: native

Iron Age: an era when people began to make tools and weapons out of iron

Jazz Age: the 1920s and 1930s, when jazz music and dance styles became popular in the United States, the birthplace of jazz

Medieval Gothic: a style of planning and designing buildings that started in France in the 1100s, spread across Europe, and lasted until the 1500s, as seen in cathedrals and castles

monarchy: a form of government with one ruler, a monarch, who often inherits the throne

nobility: high social rank, or a group of people of high birth or rank

philosophes: French for "philosophers"

Renaissance Period: "Renaissance" is French for "rebirth"; a period of about three hundred years, from the fourteenth century to the seventeenth century, during which culture, arts, and learning grew and thrived and there was renewed interest in the cultures of ancient Greece and ancient Rome

Roaring Twenties: the 1920s, a decade of cultural and economic prosperity in the United States characterized by new styles of dress and dance

robe à l'anglaise and robe à la polonaise: eighteenth-century dress styles in which a draped or split overskirt covers a large petticoat with many layers

sabot: a work shoe worn by European peasants, frequently made from a single piece of wood

siheyuan: a traditional type of Chinese residence consisting of four houses surrounding a courtyard

tartan: wool fabric with a plaid design, originally made in Scotland; the color and style usually designate a specific clan

textile: woven or knitted fabric, often used to make clothing and other household goods, such as towels, tablecloths, and bedroom linens

Tudor: a style of buildings (mainly homes) that came into fashion during the Tudor dynasty's reign in England during the sixteenth century. It combines Renaissance decorative elements and Gothic structures

turret: a small tower at the corner of a building

wayfinder: one who practices the ancient Polynesian art of ocean navigation by reading the stars, sun, and ocean swells like a map

yi-hakan: a Powhatan home like the one Pocahontas lived in

Moana

This tenacious, spirited adventurer is perfectly named: "moana" means "ocean" in multiple Polynesian languages. Though Moana's father, Chief Tui, trains her to follow in his footsteps and one day lead their island, she is called to the sea.

Origin of Story

While Moana was not a real person, her story draws on many **indigenous** Oceanian traditions. But while these island nations may be in the same part of the world, Oceania or Polynesia, each has different cultures, legends, languages, and traditions, with their own unique identity.

Historical Context

Some countries in the Pacific Ocean, such as Tonga, Samoa, and Fiji, date back to at least 1500 **BCE.** Others, like Hawaiʻi and New Zealand, weren't settled until thousands of years later. Moana's story likely would have taken place somewhere in between these periods of discovery, during a time known as the Long Pause. It's unclear why there was a gap in exploration, but one thing is for certain: Moana would have been first in line to voyage into the unknown!

Time Period: 2,000 years ago
Location: Pacific Islands

Did You Know?

While Moana's home of Motunui is a fictional island village, it was inspired by many real islands in Oceania, especially Samoa. Oceania is made up of thousands of islands!

Clothing

Because the weather in Oceania is warm year-round, clothing needs to be light and allow for easy movement. **Indigenous** people like Moana would use natural materials, such as parts of plants (fibers, leaves, flowers) to make their clothing. Adornments like what you see at the right were worn for special occasions.

Unique details, such as bird feathers, shells, seeds, and dried beans, often adorned clothing. In addition, the bones and shells from fish and shellfish could be used to make household objects, like belts or sewing needles.

Tapa example. ZiaMary / Shutterstock.com

Tapa is a type of cloth made out of the bark of a tree, such as a u'a (mulberry tree). Tools employed might include a tutua (anvil), a i'e (tapa beater), a upeti (pattern board), and a faina (small knife). Natural dyes create geometric designs and patterns.

Island Life

Motunui has many geographical features that are commonly found throughout the actual islands in the Oceania. Lining the coast of Moana's home are forests, hills, volcanoes, reefs, and beautiful beaches. The ocean is a cornerstone of life for the people who lived in the area in Moana's time.

The leader of these villages is called a chief, like Moana's father, Chief Tui. It is the chief's responsibility to make decisions that benefit the community, and to resolve any conflicts or challenges. For example, in the film, when the fishermen aren't able to catch any fish, they ask Chief Tui for advice.

Along with the chief and their family, many other people have important jobs around their village. In addition to farmers and fishermen, who provide sustenance, the village is home to storytellers, builders, clothing-makers, musicians, and tattoo artists.

Storytellers like Gramma Tala keep the past alive by sharing their customs and beliefs with younger generations. Today, different Oceanian cultures pass down their own distinct legends, mythology, folklore, and traditions in the same way.

The food Moana and her people eat comes from both the land and the sea. They enjoy fish and shellfish, as well as fruits and vegetables. They may even occasionally eat sugarcane or cacao, the seeds used to make chocolate!

Valentyn Volkov / Shutterstock.com

There are many different buildings that make up a village like Motunui. The marae is a communal gathering place in the middle of the village. Around the marae are homes called fales in Somoa and Tonga, and fares in Tahiti. They are made of various natural materials, including a foundation of rock, with walls and a ceiling made of wood, leaves, grasses, and coconut fibers.

The largest fale belonged to the village chief. This home would be centrally located and feature prominent red feathers, symbolizing royalty. Like the marae, the chief's fale would also be a place to host gatherings.

Tattoos

Tattooing in Oceanian and Maori cultures is a sacred practice that has been performed for thousands of years. Master tattoo artists pass their skill from generation to generation. Apprentices learn tattooing over many years, until they are ready to practice the art on their own.

Tattooing is a way to tell stories and impart information about one's identity, such as social status or **genealogy**, through patterns and symbols. An example of this is the manta ray tattoo on Gramma Tala's back.

Did You Know?

The pe'a is a traditional Samoan tattoo that men would have from their mid-torso to their knees!

Ancient Oceanian tattoos were done using such tools as bone, boars' teeth, turtle shells, ink, and wooden handles or mallets. The tattoo was etched into the skin by repeated tapping. The process was very painful and time-consuming—it sometimes took months to complete. Once finished, the tattoo also took a very long time to heal.

Wayfinding

The ocean beyond Moana's village reef stretches as far as the eye can see. Giant waves, storms, and predators can make a sea voyage very dangerous. Before the invention of navigational instruments like the compass and astrolabe, **wayfinders** relied on natural signs to find their way.

To follow the right path or direction, wayfinders would gaze at the sky (especially at the sun, moon, and stars) or look to the earth (following winds and currents). During their voyages, wayfinders created maps of the areas they had traveled for future reference.

Did You Know?

The main deck of voyaging canoes can be closed off–allowing for stowaways like Heihei the chicken to sneak on board!

In the film, Moana discovers a fleet of voyaging canoes in a hidden cavern on her island. Many of these canoes are double-hulled, with large outriggers (frames that extended beyond the main part of the boat). The main deck would be the primary area for seafarers to spend their time. These ships can sail long distances—perfect for brave adventurers like Moana!

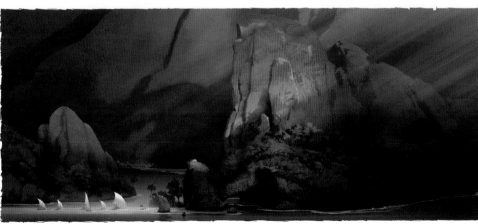

Mulan

Mulan has many wonderful characteristics, including bravery, cleverness, and loyalty. As a member of the Fa family, Mulan's name is actually Fa Mulan. In Chinese culture, the family name traditionally comes before the individual's name.

Origin of Story

The character Mulan is based on the legendary female warrior Hua Mulan. While not much is known about her life, *The Ballad of Mulan* by poet Guo Maoqian tells her story, providing us with the little information that we have. Experts believe she lived during the Six Dynasties period of Chinese history.

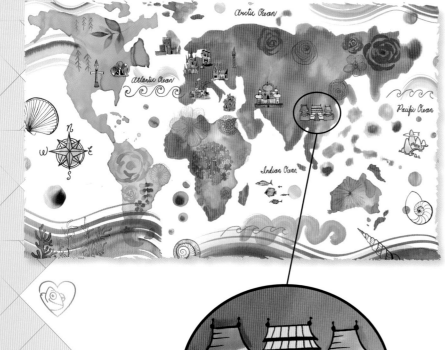

Time Period: 206 BCE–900 CE
Location: China

Historical Context

Periods in Chinese history are referred to as **dynasties**, and they are broken up by the individuals or families who ruled during each time period.

The dynasties most relevant to Mulan's story:

Han Dynasty (206 BCE–220 CE)

Six Dynasties Period (220–589 CE)

Sui Dynasty (581–618 CE)

Tang Dynasty (618–906 CE)

Did You Know?

In the beginning of the movie, we see guards patrolling the Great Wall of China, watching for enemies. At one point in history, this barricade was more than 13,000 miles long. It was constructed to protect the Chinese from outside invaders. The wall, as most people think of it today, was built during the Ming Dynasty (1368–1644 CE). Today, it serves as a symbol of China's power and history.

© Shutterstock

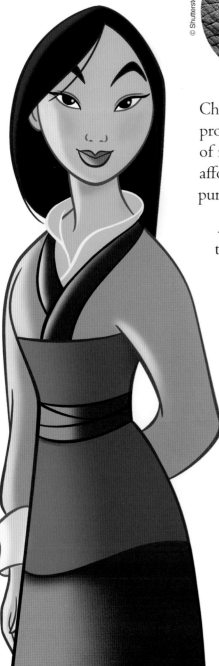

Clothing

In the film, Mulan disguises herself as a man to join the Chinese army. She wears a leather helmet and a protective covering called stone skin, which is made of rhino or buffalo leather. Stone skin was a more affordable alternative for soldiers who couldn't purchase metal armor.

As shown in the film when Mulan prepares to meet the matchmaker, it was traditional for young women in Mulan's time to apply cosmetics, or makeup, to their eyes, cheeks, and lips. Many women lightened their complexion using powder made from rice, lead, oyster shells, mother of pearl—also known as nacre—or even crushed pearls!

Women from lower classes would wear less ornate hairstyles, like a bun. More affluent women often had elaborate updos, with fresh flowers or silk, or even jade or gold accessories.

© Walt Disney Animation Research Library

Inventions and Innovations

Michael Roeder / Shutterstock.com

Many inventions from Mulan's time are still used today or are precursors of items we still use today. Paper, printing, gunpowder, and the compass are widely considered to be the Four Great Inventions of ancient China.

Compass. Andrea Paggiaro / Shutterstock.com

The compass was a useful spoon-shaped instrument invented in ancient China. A lodestone could be used to help show direction, as the stone would point south when suspended freely, due to its magnetic properties. For this reason, the compass was originally called the south pointer.

Abacus. FabrikaSimf / Shutterstock.com

Before there were calculators, people used a device called an abacus to make mathematical calculations. This invention used wooden beads arranged based on the decimal system. In fact, in the film, one of Mulan's ancestors used an abacus to calculate how much trouble Mulan is causing!

It is widely believed that an official of the Chinese **court** named Cai Lun invented paper and the papermaking process. He added such items as tree bark and old fishing nets to the existing mixture, to make paper that is more like what we have today. Eventually, this would lead to other great innovations, such as the invention of paper money.

© Walt Disney Animation Research Library

Gunpowder was invented by accident when Taoist alchemists were trying to create an elixir of immortality (the ability to live forever). They mixed saltpeter, sulfur, and carbon together, which created the chemical explosive.

Gunpowder was used to create firecrackers and fireworks. The powder went into bamboo tubes, and other ingredients were added to give color and sparkles to the display.

Fire cannons, such as the one Mulan used to create a snowy avalanche and defeat the Huns, also made use of gunpowder and bamboo tubes. In addition, soldiers could add rocks and other harmful items to the cannon to make it more dangerous.

Architecture

In the film, Mulan lives with her father, Fa Zhou; her mother, Fa Li; and Grandmother Fa in a **siheyuan**-style home, which was common during the Zhou, Han, and Tang dynasties.

The Emperor's Palace, seen toward the end of the film, was inspired by the architecture of the Tang dynasty, a period of peace and prosperity known as the Golden Age of China.

Traditions

When the Imperial Chinese Army defeats the Huns in the film, the town celebrates with a parade featuring kites, lanterns, musicians, acrobats, and a dancing lion figure. All of these are still seen in Chinese festivals today. Some examples of these celebrations are the Lunar New Year Festival, the Lantern Festival, the Dragon Boat Festival, and the Feast of the Hungry Ghosts. These occasions are a time for gathering and celebration, and an important part of Chinese culture. They can last anywhere from one day to several weeks!

Jasmine

Princess Jasmine shares her name with a beautiful, fragrant flowering plant. But unlike the jasmine flower, Princess Jasmine is not delicate. She is strong-willed, empowered, and believes that she should be free to make her own decisions. She rebels against the status quo. As a result, she changes the world around her.

Origin Story

Aladdin and Jasmine's story comes from *One Thousand and One Nights* (also known as *Arabian Nights*), a famous collection of mostly Middle Eastern and Indian tales. Over the years, these stories, written by many different authors and passed down through generations, have been compiled in various treasuries and anthologies, and have made their way into western folklore.

Did You Know?

While Jasmine's home, Agrabah, is a fictional place, it was inspired by real cities in Iran and elsewhere in the Middle East. Iran is a country in the Middle East, which is part of the continent of Asia.

Historical

Jasmine's story takes place sometime between the ninth and eleventh centuries, when new ideas and beliefs were rapidly spreading across the continent. Some areas most affected by these changes were religion, science, technology, mathematics, astronomy, and culture.

Time Period: 800–1000
Location: Middle East

Arctic Ocean

Atlantic Ocean

Indian Ocean

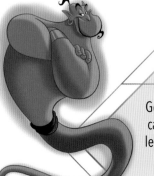

Did You Know?

Genies, called jinn, and magic carpets were popular in these legends and adventure stories.

Clothing

safakcakir / Shutterstock.com

Jasmine is often seen wearing large pieces of jewelry, such as triangular or hoop earrings, gold necklaces, and decorative headbands. It is realistic that a princess who lived during the film's time period would have owned a lot of gold jewelry, but in real life, it likely would have had more delicate or decorative touches than Jasmine's simple pieces.

The outfit that Jasmine wears into the marketplace closely resembles the authentic traditional clothing of the time. Women who lived in the Middle East between 800–1000 often wore a headscarf, known as a hijab, and a full-length outer garment, an abaya, while out in public. Many women all over the world still wear these garments today.

Stockshakir / Shutterstock.com

Muslin is a plain cotton fabric popular in warm climates. While Europeans believed the material came from Mosul, a town in Iraq, it is now believed to have originated in Bangladesh.

Did You Know?

In arid and semi-arid climates, people often wear light, loose layers to stay cool. As a princess, Jasmine has many layered outfits to choose from.

The Palace of Agrabah, Jasmine's home

Architecture

An iconic image from Aladdin is the beautiful palace of Agrabah. The palace rises prominently over the rest of the city and has many rooms, domes, and arches. As we learn from Jafar, it also has secret rooms! In addition, its sprawling gardens and grounds include a menagerie, where animals live. While Jasmine's home was not based on any particular palace, it does resemble some that exist in the Middle East.

Many examples of architecture from this time can be seen in Persian miniatures, a small, intricately detailed painting popularized during this time period. Like the image below, these tiny works of art are often characterized by elaborate scenes, bright colors, and silver and gold accents.

Persian miniature. steve estvanik / Shutterstock.com

Inventions and Innovations

Jafar isn't the only one looking for new ways to do things and make his life easier! During the time of Aladdin, many exciting developments such as the invention of Algebra and the algorithm took place that left the world forever changed.

Agrabah has many similarities to the city of Isfahan, which is culturally significant to both the time period and present-day Iran. Isfahan features Persian architecture that is evident in the grandeur of Agrabah's palace. The city is also home to the Grand Bazaar, a historical marketplace that has been there since the eleventh century!

Agrabah's marketplace

The Grand Bazaar. nlinnlin / Shutterstock.com

Did You Know?

One big difference between Agrabah's marketplace and the Grand Bazaar is that the movie's marketplace was out in the open, and the Grand Bazaar is indoors, with vaulted ceilings and intricate architectural detailing.

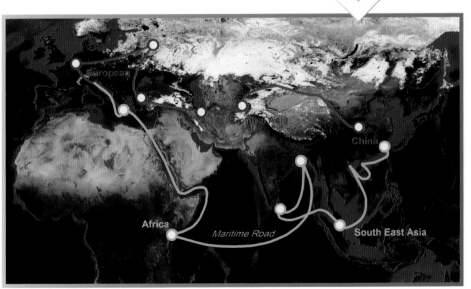

Silk Road. YIUCHEUNG / Shutterstock.com

International trade, along the Silk Road, for example, was very important during this period in history. Not only did trade routes provide access to new products, but also to new ideas and philosophies from other parts of the world. Someone like Jasmine, who is naturally curious and wants to know what lies beyond her palace's walls, would have appreciated the intellectual focus of the period.

Merida

Merida is the main character in the film *Brave*, so it comes as no surprise that she values courage. But her idea of what it means to be brave evolves throughout her story as she encounters warring clans, magic spells, and snarling bears—and ultimately, a dangerous threat to those she loves most.

Origin Story

While Merida's adventure is entirely original, the legend of the will o' the wisps she encounters has long been a part of Scottish folklore. These stories are centered around an unusual light that night travelers see flickering in the dark distance, beckoning them away from safety and toward the unknown. The lights seem to prefer swamps and marshes, which can be especially dangerous to unsuspecting wanderers. The term means "will of the torch," and science now explains that the "ghost light" is actually the result of gas emitted from decaying wetland plants!

Historical Context

The story of *Brave* takes place in Scotland during the early to middle Medieval Period, when much was changing—and declining—in Europe. This period is sometimes referred to as the Dark Ages. During this time, there was less focus on science and reason and more on magic and superstition. One well-known part of Scottish folklore is the existence and appearance of a fierce underwater creature known as the Loch Ness Monster. This legendary animal, sometimes called Nessie, is said to live in a lake called Loch Ness. The first recorded "sighting" of this beast was so long ago, it happened even before Merida's time!

Alexander_P / Shutterstock.com

Time Period: 1000s
Location: Scotland

Did You Know?

Scotland is a country with heavy rainfall and lots of islands and lakes.

Clothing

In the film, Merida's outfit for the Highland Games is a traditional dress for a noblewoman of that time, made of several tight layers: a square-necked gown, a strapless corset, and a snug **chemise**. A chemise is a smock-like undergarment worn beneath a dress to keep dirt and sweat off the exterior gown, and a corset is a structured garment that shapes the torso and supports the chest. Merida's hair is tucked into a wimple, a garment that hugs the face and neck. She wears white stockings and flat shoes that lace up to the knee. The whole outfit is tight and confining—the very opposite of what Merida likes.

Women from Merida's time wore flats called ghillies. Ghillies are still worn today by some traditional Scottish dancers. Often black and made of leather, they are similar to ballet shoes and have crisscrossed laces.

The DunBroch clan emblem features a traditional pattern known as a Celtic knot. As seen here, a Celtic knot is made up of one continuous line with no end, representing infinity and eternity in loyalty, friendship, or love.

© Shutterstock

Chemise. The Metropolitan Museum of Art, New York, Purchase, Irene Lewisohn Bequest, 2005.

Traditional Patterns

As Queen Elinor frequently reminded her daughter, customs and tradition were very important during Merida's time—and they still are today! Below are some traditional Scottish fabrics and garments that have been worn for hundreds of years.

The importance of family is a central theme in Merida's story. In her time, families were often referred to as clans. In the film, members of a clan, including Merida's triplet brothers, generally wore a specific pattern, such as the DunBroch's family tartan plaid, a swatch of which is shown here.

In the film, members of the characters in Brave wear **tartan**, or plaid. ("Plaid" can also refer to cloth or accessories that are slung over the shoulder of a kilt-wearer.) Dating back at least 3,000 years, tartans became associated with different regions, clans, military units, hunting, and formal dress over time.

A kilt, such as the one worn here by Merida's father, Fergus, is a traditional knee-length pleated skirt that Scottish boys and men wear on special occasions. It is sometimes accompanied by a cloak of the same material. Kilts are often made from wool and accessorized with a leather belt, bracelets, and a pouch known as a sporran bag.

Did You Know?

Because kilts don't have pockets, the sporran bag serves as a useful place to store small items.

Architecture

Dunnottar Castle © Shutterstock

The name of Merida's family clan, DunBroch, comes from architectural structures created during the **Iron Age**. A dun is an ancient hillside fort with walls built from stone and timber. Brochs are tall, windowless towers made from dry stonewall.

Several Scottish castles influenced the design of Merida's home. Some examples include those of Edinburgh, Dunnottar, and Eilean Donan in Scotland. Like Castle DunBroch, these castles sat high atop their hillsides.

Castle Life

Brave is set before the invention of electricity. People at that time relied on candles and torches to provide light indoors and at night. Fire helped them stay warm within the dark and drafty stone walls and was essential for cooking—though the flames could be dangerous if they got out of control. In time, for safety, kitchens would be built apart from the main living quarters.

Cleanliness during the 1000s would be very different than it is today. Without running water, keeping a body clean and tidy was much more difficult. People weren't able to shower, bathe, brush their teeth, or wash their hands regularly. In fact, not only did they not realize that handwashing prevented illness— they believed the opposite! People would often wait to bathe and wash clothes in what they believed was an effort to stay "clean."

As a princess, Merida would have had household staff to wash her clothes, bring her water for baths, and provide her with perfumes to keep her smelling nice. (But we all know that would have been less important to Merida!)

Aurora

Aurora, or Briar Rose, is a spirited dreamer. But she is not content to sit idly by and wish her life away—she makes her dreams come alive by pursuing her heart's desire.

Origin Story

Sleeping Beauty is based on the French author Charles Perrault's story "La Belle au bois dormant," which translates to—you guessed it—"The Sleeping Beauty." It is the tale of a princess who is cursed by the spell of an evil fairy who puts her to sleep for a hundred years. In response, a good fairy puts everyone else to sleep until the princess is awakened by a charming prince.

Historical Context

Time Period: 1300s
Location: Western Europe

Aurora's film, *Sleeping Beauty,* is set around the time of the Middle Ages and the **Renaissance Period**, a span of about three hundred years, during which culture, the arts, and learning grew and thrived. As a result, major advancements were made in fine art, music, and literature, as well as science, mathematics, and philosophy. Major emphasis was placed on **humanism,** the focus on the everyday lives of human beings instead of a divine or supernatural power.

© Walt Disney Animation Research Library

Clothing

While Aurora's story takes place during the fourteenth century, her look is inspired by fashion and celebrities of the 1950s, when the film was made. The influence of beloved movie icons helped shape Sleeping Beauty's appearance and clothing.

One of the most dramatic moments from the film *Sleeping Beauty* is when Aurora pricks her finger on the spinning wheel's spindle and Maleficent's curse comes true. During the time when Aurora's story takes place, developments in the field of **textiles**, or woven materials, allowed time-consuming hand spinning to be replaced by spinning machines, like the one in the film. This simplified the process for making clothes.

In addition to the arts and culture, fashion evolved during the Renaissance. Clothing colors became much more vibrant, and expensive fabrics like silk became more accessible. There was also a shift toward regal elements, such as embroidery and patterns, for those who could afford them. Many of these cloth-making techniques had long been reserved only for royalty and **nobility**!

In the 1300s, a tailored fit came into fashion. As a result, the shapeless frocks of the past were replaced with complex, form-fitting garments. Because this style exposed often more of women's collarbone and shoulders, they would often wear cloaks for modesty and warmth.

For much of her upbringing, Aurora lived as a peasant in the woods. Like other women of her station during the 1300s, her dresses would have been simple and made from natural fabrics, like linen (which comes from the flax plant) and wool (which comes from sheep). Aprons were common for protecting garments while doing chores.

Hairstyles and Headwear

Aurora's long, flowing hairstyle would have signified that she was unmarried. Once wed, women of her time traditionally wore their hair up. Headwear was also important in signifying one's status. While Princess Aurora and her mother, the queen, wore crowns, noblewomen wore fancy headdresses, like the cone-shaped hennin.

30

Cone-shaped hennin. Morphart Creation / Shuterstock.com

Architecture

Castles during the 1300s, in the **Medieval Gothic** style, boasted many impressive features. Tall **turrets**, or towers, with steep spiral staircases, allowed guards to see and defend against oncoming attackers during battle. Heavy gates and a drawbridge over a moat were designed to keep out unwanted visitors. Supports called **flying buttresses** helped fortify the exterior of buildings.

© Shutterstock

Gothic architecture can also be seen in Maleficent's castle. The exterior of her home features gargoyles, statues of monstrous figures, and a dungeon, where she imprisons Prince Phillip.

Aurora's cottage is very different from the grand castle her parents live in, but it is also representative of her time period. The cottage looks like it was constructed in the wattle and daub style, in which wood, brick, plaster, and other available materials were used to create exterior walls.

© Walt Disney Animation Research Library

Inventions and Innovations

Other developments during this time improved the quality of everyday life: the hourglass and the clock made it easier to measure time; spectacles, or eyeglasses, helped people see better; and improved armor kept knights and soldiers safer during tournaments and battles. For example, **chain mail** was replaced by plate armor made from metal and leather. This new style could also be engraved in decorative patterns!

Natalia Mikhalchuk / Shutterstock.com

Evgeniyqw / Shutterstock.com

Mr Doomits / Shutterstock.com

Snow White

Snow White is kind and gentle, with a profound love of animals and nature. She is trusting, resilient, and believes in the goodness of others. She always tries to help those around her—especially her friends the Seven Dwarfs.

Origin Story

Disney's *Snow White and the Seven Dwarfs* was based on the classic fairy tale "Schneewittchen," meaning "Snow White," by two German writers known as **the Brothers Grimm.** In this story, the Evil Queen makes several attempts to kill Snow White, including lacing her up so tightly in a bodice that she faints, harming her with a dangerous hair comb, and, of course, tricking her into eating a poisoned apple. Snow White cannot be revived until the apple is dislodged from her throat. She and the prince marry, and the prince avenges the Evil Queen at their wedding.

Time Period: 1500s
Location: Germany

Arctic Ocean

Atlantic Ocean

Pacific Ocean

Indian Ocean

Historical Context

In the 1500s, Germany was broken up into many small kingdoms. While each of these kingdoms was ruled by its own leader, like a prince or a duke, the entire territory was controlled by a central power. Together with many other territories, this land was part of the Holy Roman Empire, or the Holy Roman Empire of the German Nation.

Example of Medici collar. CPA Media Pte Ltd / Alamy Stock Photo

Clothing

While Snow White and the Evil Queen have different fashion styles, they both wear stiff standing collars with a distinctly Renaissance flair. These were known as Medici collars because they were first worn by Catherine de Medici, the Queen of France. Queen Elizabeth I of England also popularized elaborate collars in the 1500s.

Both of Snow White's outfits feature elaborate or otherwise puffy sleeves, including those in the slash-and-puff style, such as the ones on her iconic blue-and-yellow dress. Fashionable sleeves were important during the sixteenth century. In fact, dresses sometimes had detachable sleeves that allowed women to mix and match looks!

© Walt Disney Animation Research Library. Photo by Byron Cohen

The film *Snow White* was set in the 1500s, but this fair princess's costume was also influenced by women's fashion in Hollywood from the 1930s, when the movie was made. Glamorous long gowns with fine detailing were popular and worn by many celebrities of the time.

Ginger Rogers and Fred Astaire in *Swing Time*. Ronald Grant Archive / Alamy Stock Photo

Joan Crawford in *Letty Lynton*. Pictorial Press Ltd / Alamy Stock Photo

Did You Know?

Some gloves during Snow White's time had small splits in the fabric to show off rings.

Architecture

Snow White's castle may have been inspired by any number of castles in Europe, though it bears a striking resemblance to Alcázar de Segovia in Spain. The castle is famous for many reasons, one being that the front has a similar shape to the bow of a ship!

Walt Disney once visited Baden-Baden, in a place called the Dark Forest in Germany. This rich forest full of pine trees inspired much of Snow White's setting in the woods near the dwarfs' cottage.

The cottage's decor was heavily influenced by a style that was appearing elsewhere in Germany and in other parts of Europe. It is a combination of Schwarzwaldhaus, or "Black Forest house," and **Tudor** style. It featured timber framing and a steep roof thatched with straw.

The inside of the dwarfs' cottage is just as quaint as the outside, and wood carving is evident in the furniture and the walls. This form of decoration, along with engraving (cutting letters and designs into an item), was popular during the Renaissance. A number of cuckoo clocks, or kuckucksuhr, appear in the cottage. Cuckoo clocks were invented by German craftspeople and clockmakers living in Baden-Baden.

Natalia Paklina / Shutterstock.com

Mining

One of the most beloved songs from the film *Snow White* is "Heigh-Ho," which the Seven Dwarfs sing together while working in a colorful diamond mine. While this type of mining was a profession during Snow White's time, it's more likely that professionals would have been mining minerals, like copper, silver, or rock salt.

Pocahontas

Pocahontas is a strong, caring, and adventurous young leader. She is a voice of reason, and she seeks to understand different ways of life. Pocahontas is not afraid to do what's right—even if that breaks with tradition. What's more, she is based on a real person!

Origin Story

The Disney film *Pocahontas* is based on a real Powhatan Algonquian woman from the seventeenth century. While there are similarities between the adventures of the character in the film and the written accounts of the real Pocahontas, much of the true history is nuanced, unknown, and influenced by those who recorded it. One thing is certain: Pocahontas had a significant impact on history as it unfolded in North America and Europe.

Captain John Smith's 1612 map of the Chesapeake Bay region. National Park Service. Public Domain.

Time Period: approximately 1595–1617*
Location: North America

*The film *Pocahontas* begins in 1607 in London, England.

Did You Know?

Pocahontas's real name is recorded as Amonute, or Matoaka, which means "bright stream between the hills." She was nicknamed Pocahontas by those who knew her because it meant "playful one."

The Real Pocahontas

Little is known about the real Pocahontas. Most details and accounts of her life come from logs written by the English adventurer Captain John Smith, which are influenced by his European worldview.

According to these records, Pocahontas's father was Wahunsenaca (Chief Powhatan), the mamanatowick (paramount chief) of the Powhatan Chiefdom, which consisted of approximately 32 indigenous nations. Unfortunately, nothing is known of Pocahontas's mother, though the lack of her presence in these accounts possibly means she died giving birth.

Tsenacommacah, where Pocahontas lived, was referred to by the British as the New World, which is now Virginia. Pocahontas worked to ease tensions and bridge relations between her people and the newly arrived English settlers.

During her teen years, Pocahontas married Kocoum, a Powhatan man, in 1610. It is not known whether they had any children.

Relations between Pocahontas and the British settlers began to fall apart over time. While staying with another tribe, Pocahontas was kidnapped by the British when she was tricked into boarding one of their ships and not permitted to leave. She was taken to Jamestown and later Henrico (a settlement near present-day Richmond), where the British used her to secure better trade from Pocahontas's father. Chief Powhatan, who loved his daughter very much, negotiated with the English in response to her kidnapping.

While in captivity, Pocahontas learned the ways of the English. Unfortunately, Captain John Smith did not visit Pocahontas for months after she was captured. When they finally saw each other again, Pocahontas expressed anger about the way he and his fellow settlers had taken advantage of her people's friendship, land, and resources.

In 1614, Pocahontas married an English settler named John Rolfe. Her father sent a representative from their Chiefdom to attend her wedding. Pocahontas and Rolfe had one child, a boy named Thomas. Sadly, she died of an illness in 1616 while on a trip back to Virginia. Her father died shortly afterward.

Pocahontas statue in Historic Jamestowne. M. Timothy O'Keefe / Alamy Stock Photo

Traditionally, Powhatan women's hair was worn loose, like Pocahontas's, and often short, like her friend Nakoma's, as very short hair would not get caught in bowstrings. Some women also chose to wear a long plait, or braid. Powhatan men grew their hair out on the left side and shaved the right side so it would not interfere with their weapons while hunting. They may also have used feathers for decoration.

Children growing up in Pocahontas's time may have worn very little clothing, if any. During colder seasons as a child, they may have worn a sleeveless deerskin cloak called a mantle. In the film, Pocahontas wore a one-shouldered dress made of materials found in nature. Historically, she would have worn an outfit similar to this only to greet visitors to her village. Everyday clothing would likely consist of a deerskin apron.

Powhatan men wore a breechcloth, a covering like a loincloth, secured with a belt around the waist. Both women and men wore leather leggings and buckskin moccasins to protect their legs and feet from nature and the elements.

From *World-Noted Women* by Mary Cowden Clarke, 1858. Designed by Charles Staal, engraved by B. Eyles. Public Domain

Unidentified Artist copy of Simon van de Passe painting of Pocahontas. National Portrait Gallery, Smithsonian Institution; transfer from the National Gallery of Art; gift of the A. W. Mellon Educational and Charitable Trust, 1942.

One of the most prevalent images of Pocahontas was created by an artist named Simon van de Passe in 1616, shortly before Pocahontas died, although it is unclear how accurate a portrayal it truly is. A similar image of her later appeared on a commemorative five-cent postage stamp in 1907.

Village Life

A Powhatan village of this time may have had from one to two hundred homes called **yi-hakans.** These homes were built and maintained by the women in the Chiefdom. The women also may have been the owners of the homes they built. According to Captain John Smith, there were between six and twenty inhabitants in each home.

Women would do many of the everyday chores around the village, such as farming, cooking, collecting water and firewood, and caring for the children. Women would also learn skills that allowed them to make items used in and around the home, such as mats, baskets, and eating utensils. They were very talented artisans, or skilled craftspeople.

Men traditionally spent most of their time fishing, hunting for food, and protecting the Chiefdom from enemies. They also made canoes, which were important for transportation and fishing. At around ten to fifteen years old, boys would begin learning valuable hunting skills. Men also helped with the children if time allowed.

Not all of the Powhatan villagers' time was spent working. Music, entertainment, and sports were important parts of their society. Early versions of hockey, lacrosse, and footraces were popular—especially among children.

Rapunzel

Rapunzel has lots of wonderful traits that make her who she is—creative, curious, and uninhibited. She is open to all that life has to offer, even if it means leaving the safety of her tower.

Origin Story

Like many classic fairy tales, the story of Rapunzel comes from the Brothers Grimm. In the original work, Rapunzel is taken from her parents as a baby by an enchantress who raises her in a high tower. One day, a prince stumbles upon Rapunzel's tower. He begins visiting her, and they plan to marry. But Rapunzel accidentally tells the enchantress about the prince, and the old woman cuts off Rapunzel's hair and sends her away, to a desert. After much misadventure and misery, the prince and Rapunzel eventually reunite and are married.

Historical Context

The **Age of Enlightenment** took place between the 1650s and the 1780s. During this time, culture, philosophy, and education flourished throughout Europe. Philosophers promoted the idea of knowledge, exploration, and learning for all. French **philosophes** Diderot, Rousseau, Voltaire, and Montesquieu were especially influential.

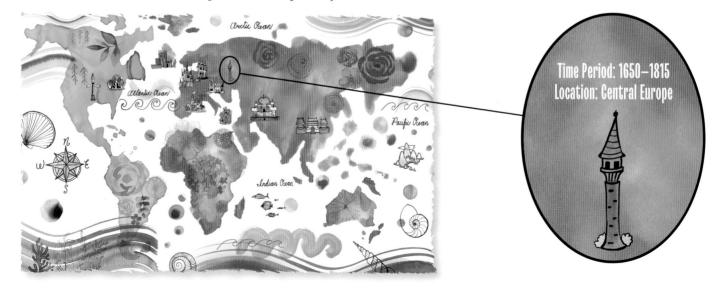

Time Period: 1650–1815
Location: Central Europe

Clothing

You may notice that several of Rapunzel's outfits feature beautiful ribbons. That's because during the time the film took place, ribbons often replaced buttons. Ribbons could be crisscrossed to secure a garment à la paresseuse, which means "in the lazy style."

Like many of the other princesses, Rapunzel's outfit features a corset. Corsets were often worn to give the appearance of a small waist, but they could be very uncomfortable and restrictive. Both men and women can wear corsets, but historically, they are mostly worn by women.

Mother Gothel is much older than she appears: she uses a magic flower to keep looking young. Fittingly, she wears clothing that reflects styles from earlier time periods than when the film was set. Her dress has bell-shaped sleeves, which were common during the Middle Ages. This is in contrast to Rapunzel's youthful style, which features lace, embroidery, and **damask** fabrics.

lynea / Shutterstock.com

Did You Know?

In the film, Rapunzel's hair is 70 feet long!

Burg Trendelburg, © Shutterstock

Architecture

In Germany, the tower of Burg Trendelburg is a real structure known as Rapunzel's Tower. This building, the main tower, used to be part of a larger castle fortress. The tower was used only for defensive purposes, as opposed to living quarters. There are 130 steps to the top!

In the film, Rapunzel's tower had a large living room, a kitchen, and separate bedrooms for Rapunzel and Mother Gothel.

The castle that Rapunzel's parents, the king and queen, reside in was heavily influenced by many real European castles. Examples include Mont Saint-Michel in France, Wawel Castle and Moszna Castle in Poland, Peleş Castle in Romania, and Kronborg in Denmark.

Mont Saint-Michel in France. Ioan-Bogdan Nechita / Shutterstock.com

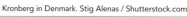

Kronberg in Denmark. Stig Alenas / Shutterstock.com

Peleş Castle in Romania. Eluhulima / Shutterstock.

Inventions and Innovations

Before Rapunzel learns that the floating lights she sees are lanterns, she thinks they are planets and stars, which she charts in her spare time. This is a nod to the science of astronomy, the study of the universe beyond Earth's atmosphere, which was advancing in this time period.

Arts and Culture

One of Rapunzel's favorite hobbies is painting. Between 1650 and 1815, there were growing opportunities in society for female artists. In Paris, France, women were being accepted into premier art programs—most notably, the Royal Academy of Painting and Sculpture—and were able to showcase their art. Women were finally being recognized for their important artistic contributions.

Self-portrait with a Monocle, 1776. Public Domain.

Some prominent female artists of the time:

- Mary Beale (1633-1699), a British portrait painter

- Anna Dorothea Therbusch (1721-1782), a Polish painter of portraits and other works (top image)

- Anne Vallayer-Coster (1744-1818), a French artist who made still-life paintings and was especially skilled at portraying flowers; she was a patron of Marie Antoinette

- Adélaïde Labille-Guiard (1749-1803), a French painter of miniatures and portraits; was an advocate for women's equality in the arts (bottom image)

- Élisabeth Louise Vigée-LeBrun (1755-1842), a French portrait painter famous for painting Marie Antoinette

Self-Portrait with Two Pupils, with Marie Gabrielle Capet (1761–1818) and Marie Marguerite Carreaux de Rosemond (died 1788). The Metropolitan Museum of Art, New York, Gift of Julia A. Berwind, 1953

Ariel

All her life, Ariel has been curious about the wide world beyond the sea. She loves exploring sunken ships, collecting human objects, and daydreaming about life on land. Her self-reliance and perseverance ultimately help her create for herself the life she wants!

Origin Story

"The Little Mermaid" was written by Hans Christian Andersen, who was born in 1805 in Odense, Denmark. He also wrote other beloved fairy tales, such as "The Snow Queen" and "The Princess and the Pea." While Andersen's original story is different from Ariel's adventure, there are certain similarities between the mermaid protagonists, or main characters. They both long for love, they strike a deal with a sea witch, they sacrifice part of themselves to become human, and they attempt to win the heart of a prince. However, while Ariel ends up happily married to Eric, Andersen's mermaid has an unfortunate fate. Her prince marries someone else, and she ultimately dissolves into sea foam.

Historical Context

Sailing the high seas was very common in the 1600s and 1700s, a time full of international travel, expansion, trade, and warfare. It's no wonder that this period was called the Age of Sail. Expansion was especially popular in European nations looking to increase the reaches of their homelands through colonization. But sea travel was dangerous. Shipwrecks, illness, and pirate attacks threatened nearly every voyage. In *The Little Mermaid* film, Ariel saves Eric from drowning when his ship catches fire and blows up during a lightning storm!

Time Period: 1600–1700s
Location: Mediterranean Sea

Arctic Ocean

Atlantic Ocean

INDIAN Ocean

N
W   E
S

Did You Know?

There are numerous examples of mermaids in legends, folklore, and popular culture. The mermaids in these stories were often tied to themes of love and immortality.

Clothing

When Ariel washes ashore for the first time, on the beach near Eric's palace, she covers herself with a sail, tying it up with rope. While her regular outfit as a mermaid consists of a seashell top that resembles a bikini, swimwear from Ariel's time was very different from what we wear today. In the 1700s, swimwear covered people from head to toe!

Did You Know?
Something Fishy
Remember Ursula's devious eels, Flotsam and Jetsam? These are actual nautical terms! **"Flotsam"** is wreckage from a ship that floats on the water. "Jetsam" refers to items thrown overboard to lighten a vessel at sea.

The pink dress Ariel wears when she is having dinner with Eric is reminiscent of other eighteenth-century dress styles, such as **robe à l'anglaise** and **robe à la polonaise**, in which a draped or split overskirt covers a large petticoat with many layers. Because layers of fabric were expensive, this type of exposed petticoat was a sign of wealth.

Ariel wears a blue ensemble on her journey through the kingdom with Prince Eric. While it may look like a dress at first glance, this outfit is actually made from several layers: a chemise undergarment, a light blue blouse, a deep blue overskirt, and a dark corset.

Ariel's small heels are similar to the 1650s style. Monarch Louis XIV of France also popularized short-heeled shoes during this time.

Robe à l'Anglaise. The Metropolitan Museum of Art, New York. Purchase, Irene Lewisohn Bequest, 1966

Treasure Untold

Ariel loves collecting gadgets and gizmos from the human world—even if she doesn't always know what they are used for. (After all, she does brush her hair with a fork after receiving misinformation from Scuttle.) But Ariel isn't alone!

Catherine de' Medici meets her sons Charles IX and Henry III, Bakalowicz, Wladyslaw (1831–1904). Heritage Image Partnership Ltd / Alamy Stock Photo

The Medicis of Italy were famous for collecting art and artifacts, and for patronizing and funding many artists and architectural developments. After many years of enjoying their vast collection privately, the last member of their family line, Anna Maria Luisa de' Medici, made their pieces available to the public which became the foundation for many museums. This started a trend that enabled many art collectors to donate works to museums for all to enjoy.

Overview of a Ship

Eric and his sailors used a ship like this one.

bow: the front of a boat

stern: the back of a boat

port: the left side of a boat

starboard: the right side of a boat

"A SHIP of War, of the third Rate," from the 1728 Cylcopaedia, Wikimedia Commons. Public Domain.

Women at Sea

Men weren't the only ones who sailed the high seas! Around the time when Ariel's film takes place, women took on the roles of sailor, shipbuilder, commander, and pirate!

Mary Lacy (c. 1740–1801) was a famous British sailor. At the age of nineteen, she ran away from home. Disguised as a boy and using the name William Chandler, she got several jobs that allowed her to work her way up in the Royal Navy. She started out as a servant, next became an apprentice, then finally a shipwright, which is a person who builds ships. When her health began to fail, she wrote a memoir about her adventures called *The Female Shipwright* so others could learn from her journey.

Mary Ann Patten (1837–1861) took over as commander of a clipper ship named *Neptune's Car* in the summer of 1856 when the captain, her husband, suddenly fell ill with tuberculosis. It was a long voyage from New York to San Francisco, but with hard work and determination, she brought the ship (and her husband) safely to their destination. As a result, she was the first woman ever to act as commander on a merchant ship—and she did it while pregnant!

Anne Bonny (c. 1698–1782) is one of history's best-known female pirates. Born in Ireland, she moved to South Carolina with her family when she was young. After refusing a suitor chosen by her father, she married another man, but ultimately left him to become a pirate and to commandeer ships, or take them over. With a band of pirates, she wreaked havoc in the Caribbean, disguising herself as a man during battles so she could fight. Eventually her pirate crew was captured, but unlike the men in her company, who were put to death, she was released and allowed to return home following her trial.

Anne Bonny. German Vizulis / Shutterstock.com

Belle

Belle's love of learning and curiosity make her open to the world and new adventures. Her perserverance helps her achieve her dreams. And she makes lots of special new friends!

Origin Story

The *Beauty and the Beast* film is based on the classic French fairy tale "La Belle et la Bête" by Gabrielle-Suzanne de Villeneuve. In French, the word for "beauty" is "belle," which explains the main character's name.

Historical Context

Belle's film takes place right before the French Revolution, a major political upheaval that had a huge impact on life throughout Europe. The reigning monarchs of France, King Louis XVI and Queen Marie Antoinette, spent money excessively, especially on clothes and furnishings at their grand Palace of Versailles. Meanwhile, the rest of the country was in a financial crisis, and ordinary French citizens were unable to buy basic necessities. This led to extreme unrest, and eventually a revolution, in 1789.

Time Period: 1700s
Location: France

Palace of Versailles. saranya33 / Shutterstock.com

Clothing

Belle's village dress, which is blue, suggests that she is not a peasant but rather a member of the merchant class. This makes sense, as her father, Maurice, is an inventor. Just like Belle, this dress is more than meets the eye. Unlike many of the other Disney Princesses, Belle would have hidden pockets in her petticoat!

Belle's iconic yellow ball gown, provided by the character Wardrobe in the film, features many of the details that were common in formal fashion of the time. Gowns were made from rich fabrics, often using metallic materials and threads that sparkled in the glowing light of a ballroom.

Hairstyles, like clothing, were also very elaborate during this period. Women, especially in the upper classes, wore their hair up. During the 1700s, some people also wore artificial hair, such as extensions and wigs.

The Metropolitan Museum of Art, New York, Purchase, Arlene Cooper and Polaire Weissman Funds, 1996

Did You Know?

The word "wig" is short for "periwig." White powdered wigs became popular during this time, as lice and medical conditions caused hair problems and baldness. But fancy wigs could be expensive! This is why the word "bigwig" is associated with importance and wealth.

Architecture

When giving Belle a tour of the Beast's castle, Cogsworth tells her, "As I always say, if it's not Baroque, don't fix it." This clever clock is talking about a period in history when décor was very ornamental, popularized by King Louis XVI of France. The Beast's castle, which is a shining example of the Baroque style, features angelic accents, fancy crests, and elegant chandeliers and candelabras—like Lumiere! The castle is similar to the famous Chateau de Chambord in the Loire Valley in France. In addition to architecture and décor, the Baroque style was also seen in the art and music of the time.

Alex Tihonovs / Shutterstock.c

Idea for an 18th century salon within the castle

The quiet village where Belle lived had different kinds of shops and tradespeople. There was a baker, a barber, a tinker (someone who mends things, like utensils), and a milliner (a person who makes women's hats). Belle's town could have been inspired by any of the small villages dotting the French countryside at this time.

Inventions and Innovations

During the 1700s, public libraries (as opposed to private libraries, like the one the Beast had in his castle) were on the rise. Books were expensive during Belle's time, so public libraries allowed working-class people the opportunity to learn new things. In addition, books were starting to be written in the languages of the people, such as French instead of Latin. As a result, there was a rise in the literacy rate, or the number of people who knew how to read and write. This would have made Belle very happy!

In the 1700s, girls were being educated for the first time, but only on certain subjects, like reading, writing, math, history, music, and needlework. Upper-class women hosted salons, or gatherings, which had both social and intellectual importance. Salons were an important way to spread new ideas.

As Lumiere explains during the "Be Our Guest" dinner scene, France is famous for its excellent food, both sweet and savory. Breads, cheeses, and pastries are some of the best-loved items produced by France, and today you can find these staples in cafés and pâtisseries, or bakeries, all over the country.

Women kicked off one of the first events of the revolution. During the 1700s, the rising cost of flour and bread caused widespread anger and panic, especially among women who were desperate to feed their families. This led to the Women's March on Versailles, the palace of the French monarchy. An unruly mob stormed the palace by the thousands and demanded to be heard by the royal family.

Women's March on Versailles, October 5, 1789. Public Domain.

Did You Know?

Before the invention of pens, people would dip a special feather called a quill into an inkwell to write.

Cinderella

Cinderella has many wonderful qualities, but one of the most admirable is her kindness toward others. She remains compassionate and full of hope even while she is experiencing neglect and mistreatment by her stepfamily. This dreamer never gives up, and in the end, her dreams come true!

Origin Story

While similar rags-to-riches folk and fairy tales have been around for thousands of years, Disney's *Cinderella* was most inspired by a 1697 book by Charles Perrault, and by *Aschenputtel*, a book by the Brothers Grimm that was published in 1812. Charles Perrault's tale, *Cendrillon ou la petite pantoufle de verre*, which means "Cinderella or the Little Glass Slipper," features the princess's iconic glass slippers. In this story, Cinderella actually attends *two* royal balls!

Historical Context

During the 1800s, a lot was happening in France. The turbulent times of the French Revolution had passed, and a new ruler, Napoleon Bonaparte, had come to power. Declaring himself emperor, Napoleon took control of the newly formed republic and began to expand French rule all over the continent of Europe. In Cinderella's time, there would have been much uncertainty about the transition from absolute **monarchy** (the rule of kings and queens), to new forms of government.

The Emperor Napoleon in His Study at the Tuileries, 1812, by Jacques-Louis David. National Gallery of Art, Washington, D.C., Samuel H. Kress Collection

Time Period: early to mid 1800s
Location: France

Clothing

When Cinderella performs her outdoor chores, such as feeding the chickens and horses, she slips into a pair of wooden clogs. These shoes, called **sabots**, were made of pliable wood. They would protect her feet from dust, dirt, and general barnyard muck!

© Walt Disney Animation Research Library

Cinderella's iconic ball gown may have been designed by her fairy godmother, but it was very much a product of the times. Her beret-style sleeves share the name of a famous French hat!

Cinderella wears several accessories to the ball, including long gloves, a headband, and a choker. Chokers were popular in the 1800s.

Cinderella's simple hair bun is called an Apollo knot. During the 1800s, women wore this style as a nod to ancient Greece and the Greek god Apollo.

High heels were not widely worn during Cinderella's time, though her shoes would have featured special details, like ribbons for lacing. That sounds much more comfortable than glass slippers for a night of dancing!

© Walt Disney Animation Research Library

Fashionable clothing has long been a sign of class and status—and not just for women. Men, like Prince Charming, wore clothing with fine detailing as well. Gold fringe decorative shoulder pieces, called epaulets, were a sign of status or indicated military rank.

Dressmaking

Today, people usually go to a store when they need to buy new clothes. But during the time *Cinderella* takes place, clothing was made in the home or tailored by a dressmaker for those who could afford it. Ready-to-wear clothing, which was made in large factories, did not come about until much later.

Who could forget Cinderella's beautiful pink dress, made lovingly with the help of her animal friends? Cinderella's dressmaking is a perfect example of her can-do attitude, problem-solving skills, and creative thinking. Even though she is treated like a servant, she tries to learn new things and practice her skills wherever possible, always making the most of what little she has. She is willing to work hard to make her dreams come true!

Cinderella's room at her stepmother's chateau

Portrait of Marie Antoinette, Élisabeth Louise Vigée-LeBrun, 1778, Kunsthistorisches Museum Vienna

Portrait of Rose Bertin, Jean-François Janinet the Metropolitan Museum of Art, New York, anonymous gift, 1924

Marie Antoinette, the queen of France before Cinderella's time, loved lavish fashion. She would spare no expense to have the finest clothing made of rich materials and intricate fabrics. Her outfits were so influential that even her dressmaker, Rose Bertin, became famous!

54

Architecture

Catherine Palace. Storm Is Me / Shutterstock.com

The story of Cinderella is timeless, and Mary Blair, an American artist, was integral to the development of the appearance of the film. Her visionary involvement influenced the whimsical look of the settings, especially the lighting of the grand palace, which has a soft but dramatic aesthetic. Mary also contributed greatly to the look of Cinderella as a character, and she helped develop the beloved princess's emotional depth and authenticity. For this and many other contributions to the Walt Disney Company, Mary was inducted as a Disney Legend.

Mary Blair in South America, 1941

During the 1800s, the Rococo style, which stemmed from the ornamental Baroque style, was prevalent in homes of the wealthy. Specifics of this style include asymmetry, flowing lines, and elaborate detailing, especially with an emphasis on nature. Wavy and scroll-like shapes were popular as well. Rococo style can be seen both in the Prince's castle and in Lady Tremaine's chateau.

© Walt Disney Animation Research Library

Tiana

Chronologically, since her film takes place in the 1920s, Tiana is the most modern princess. She also displays a contemporary outlook when it comes to life and love; she takes action to pursue her goals. Her hard work pays off—she becomes a chef in her own restaurant and makes her dreams a reality!

Origin Story

The Princess and the Frog is based on the beloved fairy tale "The Frog Prince," which has been around for hundreds of years. It is told in different ways all over the world, with one especially famous version being *The Frog King or Iron Heinrich* by the Brothers Grimm. But the original story of Tiana's adventure was inspired in part by a real chef named Leah Chase! Keep reading to learn more about this inspirational icon.

Historical Context

In 1802, the United States bought the territory of Louisiana from France for $15 million in an exchange that came to be known as the Louisiana Purchase. Louisiana became a state a decade later, in 1812, and New Orleans became its biggest city.

A century later, New Orleans had evolved into a rich and culturally diverse city. The city had maintained distinct French influences, especially regarding language, food, and architecture. Tiana's story takes place during this time, the 1920s, also known as the **Roaring Twenties.** This backdrop of vibrant art, jazz, and dance cultures—as well as a period of sweeping social change—made it an especially exciting time to be in America.

Louisiana Purchase Treaty of 1803 is contained in the ornate jacket.
Everett Collection / Shutterstock.com

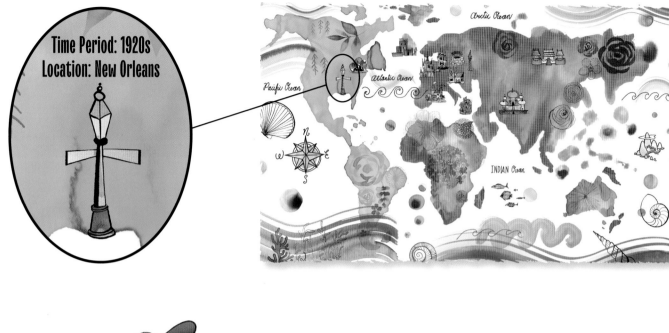

Time Period: 1920s
Location: New Orleans

Leah Chase

Tiana's character was greatly inspired by Leah Chase (1923–2019), a famous African American chef and entrepreneur. Leah's famous restaurant, Dooky Chase, was named after her husband, a local jazz musician.

In addition to the people of New Orleans, this "Queen of Creole Cuisine" fed many celebrities and politicians throughout her life, including Rev. Dr. Martin Luther King Jr., musician Nat King Cole, and President Barack Obama. She also shared her delicious cooking with the film team for *The Princess and the Frog*!

For much of Leah's life, the United States was segregated, which meant businesses were allowed to openly discriminate against specific racial groups, particularly African Americans, and not allow them to enter certain establishments. This form of discrimination, legal at the time, affected daily life everywhere, including in stores, restaurants, and schools, on public transportation, and even in bathrooms and at water fountains.

Leah Chase was an important figure in the civil rights movement, a movement in American history that aimed to end segregation—and all racial discrimination—and grant equal rights to all people. Her restaurant became a frequent gathering place for leaders to meet and discuss their plans in the fight for equality.

Leah was also very passionate about art, and used her restaurant as a gallery. She made everyone feel welcome, and brought people together with her delicious cooking. Leah has been nationally recognized with many awards and accolades for her cooking and her contributions to the Civil Rights movement. Her restaurant is now a city landmark.

Clothing and Hairstyles

Fashionable headwear, such as Tiana's bell-shaped hat, was very popular during the 1920s. This hat is called a cloche, which means "bell" in French. Other styles popular at the time were headbands and aigrettes, which are feathers or similar decorations worn in the hair. Art Deco style, including geometric patterns, was especially popular for clothing and accessories.

Ever wonder what the tall white hat that chefs wear in the kitchen is called? It's a toque blanche, which means "white hat" in French. These hats are still worn today.

As shorter dresses became more popular, so did shorter hair. The 1920s saw the introduction of the bob, a chin-length style that was radically different from what previous generations of women had worn. Bangs, or fringe, were also very popular, as were kiss curls, locks of hair styled in elegant circular shaped swirls that framed the face.

The 1920s also saw Marcel waves and finger waves, in addition to short, straight bob cuts. Annie Turnbo Malone launched the African American beauty and cosmetic industry in the 1890s when she developed a hair-straightening solution geared toward African American women. Annie Malone gave Madam C.J. Walker her first job in hair care, and became a philanthropist and educator, helping to popularize schools for cosmetology where people trained professionally to style and care for hair, skin, and nails.

During the 1920s, a new generation of liberated young women were entering the social scene. Known as flappers, these women challenged the old-fashioned rules and conventions of society. They also embraced the new culture of fashion, wearing slit skirts, fringed dresses, and low-cut shoes with straps called Mary Janes.

Did You Know?

Kiss curls were also called spit curls because people sometimes used saliva to hold the shape!

Did You Know?

The city of New Orleans is nicknamed "The Big Easy" due to the laid-back lifestyle many of its residents enjoy. It is also called NOLA, which stands for New Orleans, Louisiana. (The state of Louisiana is abbreviated as LA!)

New Orleans

Founded by a French prince in the eighteenth century, New Orleans has a unique style and architecture all its own. The French Quarter resulted from both French and Spanish influences. Buildings were made of brick and plaster, with ornamental ironwork on street-facing balconies.

The Ninth Ward, where Tiana is shown in the film to live with her parents, Eudora and James, was also the home of jazz legend Louis Armstrong, gospel singer Mahalia Jackson, and musician and singer-songwriter Fats Domino. Along with many restaurants and businesses, the Ninth Ward featured single-story row houses that attracted European immigrants and African Americans in search of affordable housing. The area was a center of rich cultural diversity.

Mardi Gras, or Fat Tuesday, is a citywide celebration that takes place every year in New Orleans (as well as other parts of the United States and around the world). In addition to eating and drinking, the holiday is celebrated with festive parades, floats, colorful confetti, bead necklaces, and masquerade balls.

Traditional dishes popular in New Orleans include gumbo, étouffée, po' boys, and jambalaya, which often feature spices, meat, shellfish, vegetables, and rice. Of course, no meal would be complete without beignets, a deep-fried dough pastry, for dessert!

Gumbo. Linda Hughes Photography / Shutterstock.com

Étuffée. Aimee Lee Studios / Shutterstock.com

Beignets. Darryl Brooks / Shutterstock.com

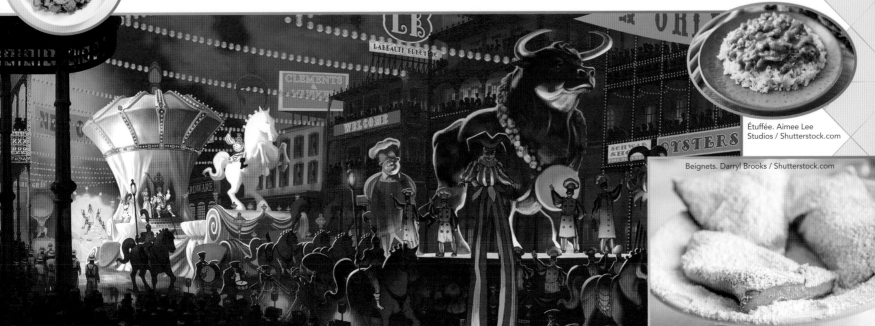

Inventions and Innovations

Music and dancing were popular forms of entertainment during the 1920s and 1930s, now known as the **Jazz Age**. This era saw the proliferation of jazz, swing, and big-band ensembles, with iconic bandleaders like Duke Ellington, singers like Ella Fitzgerald, and trumpeters like Louis Armstrong.

Duke Ellington. Photo 12 / Alamy Stock Photo

Portrait of Ella Fitzgerald, New York, N.Y., ca. Nov. 1946. Public Domain.

Louis Armstrong. GL Archive / Alamy Stock Photo

Langston Hughes. Everett Collection Inc / Alamy Stock Photo

Alain Locke: *The Broad Ax.* (Salt Lake City, Utah),
13 Jan. 1912. *Chronicling America: Historic American
Newspapers.* Lib. of Congress. Public Domain.

Zora Neale Hurston. Science History Images / Alamy Stock Photo

New Orleans wasn't the only hot spot during this time period. New York City was flourishing with the Harlem Renaissance, a period when African American writers, artists, musicians, and philosophers made celebrated contributions to entertainment and culture, receiving widespread and mainstream acclaim. Writers such as Langston Hughes, Zora Neale Hurston, and Alain Locke made especially valuable contributions to literature, which are still read to this day.

Following World War I, more and more women were empowered to pursue their passions and interests outside the home. New educational options, career prospects, and property rights for women also created new opportunities for them to succeed. Some career women even started their own businesses and became entrepreneurs, like Annie Malone and Madam C.J. Walker introduced earlier. Their innovative hair care products for African American women revolutionized the world of cosmetology. Their hard work and business savvy led them to both become self-made millionaires!

Did You Know?

Do you know all the words to your favorite movie? If so, it might surprise you that before the 1920s, movies were silent! They had no dialogue, or talking, due to the limitations of the technology. With advancements in the entertainment industry, talking movies, or "talkies," were produced.

Annie Malone, the University of Missouri Saint Louis Black History Project Collection. Public Domain.

Afterword

As you've learned throughout this book, no two Disney Princesses look, speak, or act the same. Their stories take place all over the world, both on land and deep in the ocean. They wear different clothes—soldiers' armor, dazzling ball gowns, and even beach clothes! Some journey on horseback, like Belle; others hike through snowcapped mountains, like Mulan; and others sail across the ocean, like Moana!

Just as there are many different ways to be a princess, there are many different ways to be a leader. The Disney Princesses were leaders during their times, and the future needs people like you to make the world a better place for everyone.

One thing all leaders have in common is they are sometimes faced with difficult challenges. Just think of the challenges the Disney Princesses endured! But a real leader thinks outside the box to find solutions and overcome obstacles. When you put your mind to something, anything can happen!

You already have everything inside you to make history and change the world. All you need is the courage to lead, and a willingness to work hard to make your dreams a reality. Surround yourself with people who support you, like family and friends who can help you live up to your full potential.

Tiana

Merida

Mulan

Aurora

Snow White

Rapunzel

Ariel

Pocahontas

Jasmine

Like the Disney Princesses, do your best to find joy in every day and embrace what you love. And remember: don't compare yourself to others, because no one else has the same journey— it's up to you to create your destiny!

So, what are you waiting for?

Adventure awaits!

Belle

Moana

Cinderella

For Mikayla,
my brave and clever princess
—C.B.C.

Front cover art: Chemise from The Metropolitan Museum of Art, New York, Purchase, Irene Lewisohn Bequest, 2005. Neuschwanstein Castle used under license from Shutterstock.com. All other art © Disney Enterprises, Inc.

Back cover art: Isfahan Grand Bazaar used under license from Shutterstock.com. *Women's March on Versailles* is in the public domain. All other art © Disney Enterprises, Inc.

Production artwork from the Walt Disney Animation Studios, courtesy of the Walt Disney Animation Research Library.

rhcbooks.com
ISBN 978-0-7364-3939-8 (trade)
MANUFACTURED IN CHINA
10 9 8 7 6 5 4 3 2 1

Random House Children's Books supports the First Amendment and celebrates the right to read.